GATES

OF WORSHIP

ANDREW ALLANS MUTAMBO

GATES OF WORSHIP

Rivendell Publishing

www.rivendellpublishing.com

Illustria Design

LAYOUT & COVER DESIGN
Anthony Saint for Illustria
Nairobi, Kenya
+254 722 102232
tony.saint30@gmail.com

To order copies online visit:
Andrewmutambo.com
Or by mail contact:
Pastor Andrew Mutambo
P.O BOX 22292
Kampala, Uganda.
U.S (Google line): 1-804-601-0394.
Ugandan (Mobile line) : +256-772-404389
Email: andymutts@gmail.com

Dedication

I owe everything about this book to the great King and Father of all, for the grace and inspiration about worship that He has put on my heart for my generation. For all who chance to read this book, may the good Lord awaken and stir your heart to deeper dimensions of worship. Let the King of glory rejoice over you with singing.

In addition, my parents have been my role models from a tender age. Dad has always encouraged me to go higher, while Mum has often been the soft spoken prophet in my life. Thank you, dad and mum, for the nurturing work you have done in me. Most of the principles you taught me are still sustaining me to this day. I dedicate this book to you as well.

Acknowledgements

My sincere thanks and gratitude go to Dr. Bill Jackson, retired professor of the University of Virginia for the time he has put in editing my manuscript.

To my fellow pastors' in Revived Glory Church, thank you for your continuous encouragement, love, prayers and for allowing me time to pursue this dream and its authorial formulation. And to my Church family, my sincere gratitude for your love, support and patience during the times of separation and study in the course of writing my books. You are the wind beneath my wings.

My thanks as well go to Pastor Duke Chance of New Life Church, Louisiana whom I recently met and who, with his sincere, humble and loving fatherly heart, has become an integral part of my life. Apostle Charles Tumwine, I commend you for being my counselor and true friend. Pastor Danny Mbako, as a longtime friend turned brother, your words of encouragement have become bench marks in my life.

Forward by Harold Bare

Several years ago I met Andrew Mutambo. My first impressions were of an apt young man with social skills to be negotiable in international ministry. He is sensitive to counsel, insightful and devoted to Kingdom work. His Love for people is evident. His desire to pastor and contribute to skill development of pastors is passionate.

When he submitted this manuscript on worship to me I chose to vet it with an esteemed theologian, who is a colleague. The scholarly review that came back to me was most affirmative that Andrew's efforts would be a contribution to those who have a true heart for worship.

Harold L. Bare, Sr., Ph.D.
Senior Pastor
Covenant Church
Charlottesville, VA, USA

Introduction

City gates are mentioned many times in the Bible particularly in the Hebrew Old Testament. In Bible times a gate was the center of city life. Originally designed to defend a city against attack, this massive structure soon became a combination of community center, city hall, and marketplace. People paid their taxes in the city gate, officials settled legal matters there, prophets prophesied and kings ruled in the gate.

In the Ancient Near East city gates were neither merely entrances, nor only used for military protection. As a potentially weak point in the defenses, the gates of walled cities typically had three chambers giving four sets of "doors" and defended spaces between.

The chambers were roofed and made available

for use as public buildings. It is likely that these chambers served as "offices" for city administration. In the space outside the gate, market stalls would have been erected, as they are today. The "gate" was therefore the marketplace where traders and peasants met with city folk to sell and exchange goods.

Inside the gateway, a space was left without buildings which served as a communal area for meetings and public justice. Just inside the gate at Dan, in Israel, for example, there is a raised dais that had provision for a canopy to be erected. This would have served as the judge's throne. The shops and markets around the gate provided for the people's daily needs.

Lot sat in the gate of Sodom. In the gate, Boaz established his legal right to marry Ruth. Absalom won the affection of Israel in the gate. The Bible also predicts the return of the Messiah for the Last Judgment in the symbolism of the Eastern Gate of Jerusalem.

Gates also played a distinct role in times of war and subsequent victories. It was characteristic of conquering kings to ride back through their kingdom gates with pomp, valor and glamour after a massive conquest. Often times the battles lasted months or a year. The kings came back, decked in long trains/robes symbolic of their victory, bringing captives and spoils of war from conquered cities and kingdoms. These 'trains' were emblems or robes stripped from the conquered kings.

The city was adorned in preparation for the king's return. Bells rang and trumpets sounded to announce his arrival. Citizens of the kingdom, eager and zealous to see their long absent and returning king, paraded on the king's-highway. Others awaited him on walls or rooftops, waving and chanting slogans of praise for him. It was a time of celebration and feasting, and often times the king threw a party for his high palace officials, generals and even his citizens as a whole. The feast often lasted days or weeks.

This metaphor typifies the Christ King after he had finished his work on earth, ascending into heaven and being welcomed through the Celestial gates by an innumerable company of angels. It also depicts our Redeemer-King making his entrance into the lives of his people through the gates of their hearts. It is said, heaven goes into celebration-mode when one soul accepts the Lordship of Christ Jesus.

In this book, I endeavor to define the Gates of Worship, communicating chapter by chapter what it takes for the King of Glory to stride through them and what transpires when they are made available for his purpose.

TABLE OF CONTENTS

Chapter One

AN OUTLOOK ON GATES

Friends, in our study about 'gates of worship', we will focus on the Christ King making his entrance into our lives on a continuous basis. Paul while writing to the Philippians says, *'work out your salvation with fear and trembling'*. Our 'work out' centers on making the most of the avenues God has created in us that warrant his entrance into our lives daily. As previously noted, conquering kings of old easily, freely and blissfully strode through the gates of their kingdoms because of the warranted reception of their subjects. After being out for long periods in the heat or cold of battle, they anticipated and deserved a hero's reception. The welcome was always rapturous, assuring them of the undying loyalty, love and admiration of their citizens.

Amidst the diverse biblical meanings and usages of the word 'gate', my usage is drawn from the Hebrew word 'deleth' meaning 'gate or door', which words I will use together or interchangeably. Through our conversation, we will discover that our lives are prototypes of gated cities.... but as Cities of God. The scripture below likens you to a vibrant and blooming city whose interior and gates are buzzing with activity.....to the glory of God.

Mathew 5:14
Ye are the light of the world. A city that is set on an hill cannot be hid.

Earthly kings returning with loot and spoils of war often times distributed a good chunk amongst their generals and men of war and put the rest into kingdom coffers. Likewise God never comes to his people empty handed. That is why the Prophet Isaiah declares, *"oh that you would tear the heavens and come down so that the mountains would quake at your presence. When you did awesome deeds that we expected"* (Isaiah 64:1-3).

When he descends from his throne, He does so with diverse packages for His people; and that is after a well fought battle and secured victory by His saint-soldiers. The battles we wage, with Him as captain of our salvation, may take days, months and years; but payday always comes around AND God makes good on his word.

The cities of old had gates/doors that provided access to the inner and innermost sections of the kingdom. Within the kingdom, there were the king's palace(s), places of worship, houses for kingdom officials, possibly a coliseum, prison cells and buildings for different purposes and uses. These were often big and with many access doors and routes. The king had the prerogative of utilizing any entry point at any time in his kingdom, by virtue of his sovereignty and Lordship. In like manner, as Cities of God, Jesus has the right of entrancing into every segment of our lives because he is King and Lord. The catch is, He would love to do so by invitation! He never forces his will on us, but as we endeavor to fling our gates open, He steps in.

The anatomy of the biblical passage below reveals a vivid picture of our King entering through the gates of his domain. Walk with me through the next chapters of this book as I attempt to interpret the sequence of events; examining verse by verse how it all fits together.

Psalms 24:6

This is the generation of them that seek him, that seek thy face, O Jacob.

Psalms 24:7

Lift up your heads, O ye gates; and be ye lift up, ye everlasting doors; and the King of glory shall come in.

Psalms 24:8

Who is this King of glory? The LORD strong and mighty, the LORD mighty in battle.

Psalms 24:9

Lift up your heads, O ye gates; even lift them up, ye everlasting doors; and the King of glory shall come in.

Psalms 24:10

Who is this King of glory? The LORD of hosts, he is the King of glory.

Chapter Two

WORSHIP, A DEFINITIVE PURSUIT OF GOD

Let us begin with the sixth verse which mentions two words; 'generation' and 'seek'. The generation mentioned isn't a period of time that was specifically tied to a people living during that epoch, but any passage of time and a people living in it. The Bible will always speak to us in the now because it is the living word of God. Therefore as you and I read it, the generation being addressed is the present. The other word is 'seek'. When translated from its Hebrew root word, it means, *'to tread or frequent, to follow, strive or search...*

specifically to worship.' We are living in a time and age when God is restoring the fallen tabernacle of David.

Amos 9:11
In that day will I raise up the tabernacle of David which is fallen, and close up the breaches thereof; and I will raise up its ruins, and I will build it as in the days of old:

Amos 9:12 (1889 Darby Bible)
that they may possess the remnant of Edom, and all the nations upon whom my name is called, saith Jehovah who doeth this.

Folks, this is the day and age in question. As that tabernacle was without partitions but only the place of the Ark, He longs to see scores of humble and genuine hearts yearning to throng before him in worship without any spiritual red-tape, religious bigotry or spiritual bureaucracy. With His people engulfed in such passion and drive, we will begin affecting the un-churched and those around us, causing a crowding of the nations into His kingdom.

Now, understanding the heart of God and discerning the tenderness of the hour, will birth a pursuit in your heart for Him. You will also discover in the same verse (Psalms 24: 6) that, *it is his face that is sought*...NOT his hand as many are doing in our Churches. This has produced a lot of stunted and self centered Christians. When you purpose to see ones face, it either means it's been long since you beheld them and you desire to know their state of affairs OR you miss and love them so much that you would savor being with them. That is what the Psalmist meant in the sixth verse by, *'this is the generation that seeks thy face'*.

Are you willing to be that generation, Child of God?

Emphasis in some churches and places of worship has been placed on a receive it, name it and claim it gospel. These things in themselves may not be wrong, but stress has been placed on the secondary and not the primary object..... which is Christ in us the hope of glory! We have ended up putting the cart before the horse and thereby misdirected our focus.

It is documented that in some parts of the world, especially where Christianity faces mounting persecution and opposition, that there is such a hunger and craving for God that makes them pursue Him to extents where miracles have become *'daily food for the children'* as the Bible declares. Do you not marvel that in one part of society people are fervently seeking miracles and in another part miracles are following them! Where have we gone wrong, friends? Where did we veer off the path?

Jeremiah 6:16
This is what the LORD says: "Stand beside the roads and watch. Ask for the ancient paths, where the good way is. Walk in it and find rest for yourselves. But they said, 'We won't walk in it!'

The difference is, worship is about seeking to behold His face, prayer is about seeing His hand move on your behalf. Now, it is a mark of a true worshipper to move from a level where you are not just interested in seeing his hand work in your life to a level of striving, panting and desiring to behold his beauty and splendor. You begin seeking God for who He is, not what

He has; not what you get from him, but what he gets from you. Because in worship, **God is the audience and we are the auditioners,** as I write in one of my books, *Worship Keys for Worthful Living.*

You and I should pattern our lives after David, who every morning set aside a time to sing aloud of his mercies. When you examine the life of this great King, you will notice that it was punctuated with battles for nearly half of his lifetime. Yet his harp was closest to him during his dire moments. I encourage you to develop a daily habit of ascribing greatness to the king whether things are working in your favor or not. That is a litmus test of a true worshipper and a challenge to demonstrate before your God that your love for Him is greater than your need. Believe you me, it will be foundational to the King's entering and seeing your gates of worship fully operational.

Psalms 59:16

*But I will sing of thy power; yea, I will sing
aloud of thy mercy in the morning: for thou
hast been my defense and refuge in the day of
my trouble.*

We all recall one of the greatest trials ever
recorded in history, when in the wee hours
of the morning, Abraham is awakened by a
voice telling him to go offer his only Son Isaac
on a mountain that will be told him. Without
question and hesitation, he sets out on a three
day journey to fulfill this divine command. It
must have been one of the longest trip of his
lifetime because it was filled with questions,
queries and quagmires; but he kept moving.
Fast forwarding to the climax of the story, he
returns with the lad just as he told the young

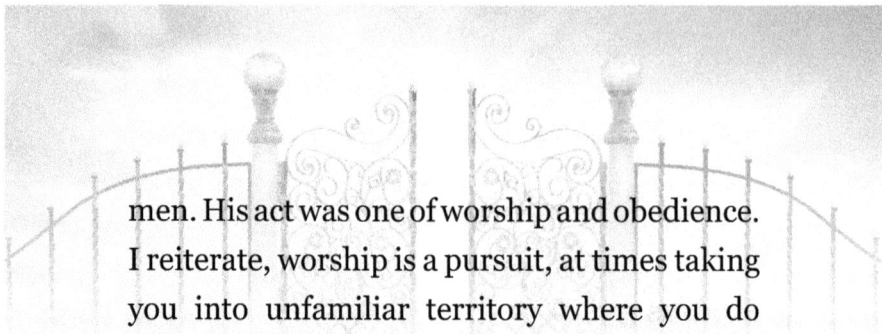

men. His act was one of worship and obedience. I reiterate, worship is a pursuit, at times taking you into unfamiliar territory where you do things that are beyond the norm. *It is only when men begin to worship that they begin to grow. Calvin Coolidge (1872–1933).*

Genesis 22:5

And Abraham said unto his young men, Abide ye here with the ass; and I and the lad will go yonder and worship, and come again to you.

Chapter Three

KINGS' RESPOND TO ACKNOWLEDGEMENT

Kings by virtue of their position and status will always respond to acknowledgment. Meaning, when their subjects recognize and heap praises on them for their rule, influence, power, love and dominion, they respond by lavishing on them blessings, goods and property, and in some cases pardon to convicted felons. In some cultures, kings have been known to give lands, daughters and material wealth to their loyal subjects. This is often after a subject's amazing display of love.

I come from an African background where kings have been an integral part of history. One evening, as custom was, during one of our great family gatherings, while seated by a bonfire, my granny tells a story of how our king's of old during their occasional visits to areas in their domain and being welcomed by the locals never allowed their spears to rest directly in the ground. Someone had to volunteer his foot to be pierced right through. On many of these brave, loving and loyal subjects, lands and gifts were lavished by the King. Notice how crude and painful the act used to be, though very rewarding. Thanks be to God, we do not have to endure such an ordeal to win our King's affection!

The gospel of Mark records a story of a display of love. Salome a daughter of Herodias, the wife of Herod, came in and danced before him during his birthday. Herod was much pleased by what she did for him in the presence of his officials and told her to ask for anything, even up to half of his kingdom. Overwhelmed by the offer, she hastily runs to her mother to seek counsel on what can best suit her given the open invitation of her father. We all know how the story ends. Folks, kings are moved by affection.

The key to this is mentioned in the opening words of the seventh and ninth verse of Psalms 24. *'Lift up your heads, O ye gates'*. A 'head' in scripture is a symbol of authority, honor and rank. A man is the head of a home, Christ is the head of the church. We see this recurring in human and animal life, a system ordained of God from beginning of time. The second bit of the verse says, '....and be ye lifted up'.

The word 'lift up' means, 'to magnify, respect, regard and receive'. Now this is where it gets interesting, folks.

Before our king can come into the gates, the 'heads' have to be 'lifted up'. The worship principle here is the relinquishing by the people of authority, rank and honor to a higher and greater one, one with more authority, that is to the King of glory. And doing it with the respect, regard and deep reverence they have for Him, will obligate Him to come through the gates of their lives. (I will share in detail the meaning of gates in the final chapter).

Remember, kings respond to acknowledgment! Through my travels I have seen and learned from different cultures and am still doing so.

One time while in South Africa on a mission trip, I visited a Zulu couple that had invited me for dinner. It was a weekend and I was casually dressed. I walked through the door with a cap on my head. I did not know until I was told later that in their culture, it is disrespectful for a guest to walk into another man's house with a hat on his head. I have also had the chance to interact with some Orientals, among whom bowing the head is a sign of sincere respect for a guest, practiced by female and male hosts.

The lifting up of our heads is a metaphor, a spiritual symbol, of an act through which we show our supreme respect and reverence before God, our greatest Guest. The quiet times of worship we set aside for Him in our homes OR during a public worship gathering should underscore the principle of 'lifting up'

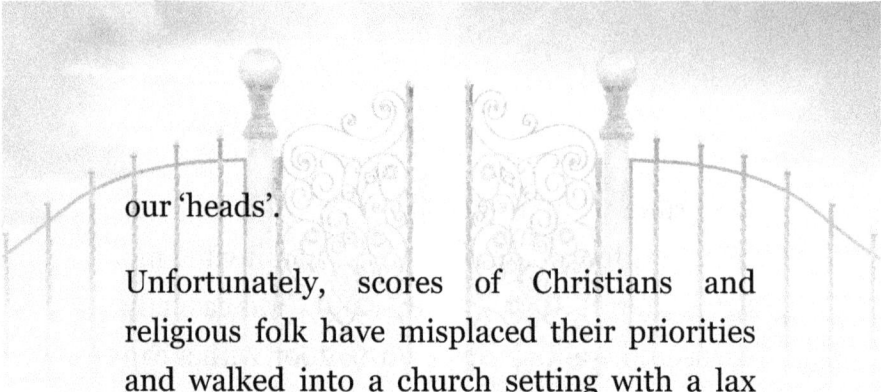

our 'heads'.

Unfortunately, scores of Christians and religious folk have misplaced their priorities and walked into a church setting with a lax and disrespectful attitude, tone and act. If we keep coming before God with these negative inclinations, social bias, ego and unbalanced mindsets, we will hardly, I repeat hardly, see him come through our gates. Our God is a jealous God!

Exodus 34:14
For thou shalt worship no other god: for the LORD, whose name is Jealous, is a jealous God:

Don't forget, whatever takes up our mind and time as a priority, is a god. Thus as the passage suggests, we should 'lift up' (receive, regard and respect) our 'heads' (our honor, rank and authority) to God alone with a fervent concentration on him. In addition, going to a church service having your head stooped or bowed low because of what has transpired in the day or week is depictive of surrendering your authority and honor to self. Self in all its forms whether self-pity, self-righteousness, self gratification, etc, is the strongest demi-god one can entertain. It is an attitude of ingratitude and insubordination before your King. It shows conclusively that you are magnifying yourself and your circumstances above the Eternal Being you presume you have come to meet. It grieves His heart to see that you are approaching Him with a spirit of heaviness or a grumpy attitude.

The present church should emulate the early church by getting back to the place of putting God in 'expectation-mode'. Whenever they gathered for fellowship, they did it with joy, simplicity of heart and praising God, Who added to their fellowship such as should be saved. In other words their actions set in motion sporadic miracles and visitations of God on unprecedented levels. We can choose to have the same experience of God in our spiritual gatherings.

Psalms 34:1
I will bless the LORD at all times; his praise will be in my mouth continually.

Psalms 34:2
My soul will glorify the LORD; the humble will hear about it and rejoice.

Psalms 34:3
Magnify the LORD with me! Let us lift up his name together!

Psalms 34:4

I sought the LORD and he answered me; he delivered me from all of my fears.

Psalms 34:5

Look to him and be radiant; and you will not be ashamed.

Chapter Four

KINGSHIP ATTRIBUTES UNFOLD WHEN GATES OPEN

Steadily and systematically through our scriptural passage (Psalms 24), we are seeing a process building up to the King's entrance into the gates. This time, it is His attributes that unfold as He makes his way. Verse eight and ten attest to it. A question is posed, *who is this king of glory?* Answers are given to the effect, *'the LORD strong and mighty, the LORD mighty in battle, the LORD of Hosts, he is the king of glory.'* You will discover in these two verses that some attributes of God are mentioned, inferring that, the moment we acknowledge (worship) God with deep respect and reverence, He will stride through our lives revealing and manifesting different aspects and features of His personality.

In the unfolding of his attributes, the word LORD is used. Translated from its original Hebrew, it is 'Yahweh', a name the children of Israel dared not mention for fear of desecrating it. The Old Testament writers preferred Jehovah. The name Jehovah is first mentioned in the book of Exodus when God is making Himself known to Moses and 'carving out' for himself a people from among the nations. It is therefore a relational name that identifies God with his chosen ones.

When God calls Abraham and speaks to him in

the twilight, He tells him to look and see if he can number the stars in the sky and sand on the sea shore. Child of God, there are two sets of children being addressed. The stars in the sky speak of the spiritually begotten children of Abraham which is you and me, while the sand of the sea speaks of the natural born nation of Israel. Therefore the name LORD is relational, meant to be used by someone close and dear to him, that is, a child of God.

The eighth verse reads, *the LORD strong and mighty, the LORD mighty in battle.* This is one of the attributes revealed by the King on His way through the gates. The writer of this Psalm may have been experiencing physical or emotional battles AND needed his God to show up. David was a man of battles throughout his lifetime but God always came to his rescue.

He was a man of many enemies because of his many exploits. In this scenario, he needed a manifestation of a warrior king in his life. In the course of his worship, David envisages his king as the LORD strong and mighty, the LORD strong in battle. In his 'world' or present situation, this manifested attribute was a Rhema (specific word for his need).

Friends, like David we experience life's battles on different spectrums. Some are financial, emotional, domestic, work related, health concerns and so on. Through our worship, God will show up on our level and manifest His attributes. For someone venerating Him as a Healer, He will show up as Jehovah Rophe; to the one seeking (worshipping) Him as Provider, He will reveal Himself as Jehovah Jireh; to the one magnifying Him for His mercy and grace, He will disclose Himself as Jehovah Tsidkenu.

Recall the words He spoke to Moses by the burning bush when asked for His name. He declares, tell the children of Israel, I Am has sent you. I Am your source, I Am your joy, I Am your health, I Am your protector, I Am your exceeding great reward. Whatever you worship Him as, the I Am will be to you.

Exodus 3:13

Moses told God, "Look, when I go to the Israelis and tell them, 'The God of your ancestors sent me to you,' they'll say to me, 'What is his name?' What should I say to them?"

Exodus 3:14

And God said unto Moses, I AM THAT I AM: and he said, Thus shalt thou say unto the children of Israel, I AM hath sent me unto you.

If we are to do a prognosis on the two verses eight and ten and imagine we needed the same attributable experience of God as David had, this would be my zoomed in version of the outcome.

a) As LORD strong and mighty....you would see your Warrior King flexing His muscle and revealing His power by speaking to the raging storms of your life, 'peace be still'.

b) As LORD mighty in battle.....you would behold him as the ever present skilled Fighter having mastery over your foes in battle. A Conqueror and undisputed Champion who never loses and has never lost a single battle.

c) As LORD of Hosts....you would envision him as the Commander in Chief, the General over his army. Our God commands a vast army of saints and angels. He has tactfully positioned them in two realms, earth and heaven. The latter often join forces with the former to set in order the affairs of the earth realm. Joshua espied Him as the captain of the host of the LORD. He never leaves a man behind, neither does He abandon His troops. The scripture says they all came out of Egypt and all crossed the red sea. Through the ages, he has led his armies of saints and angels to successive victories. What an Icon, what a leader!

Exodus 15:3
The LORD is a man of war: the LORD is his name.

Psalms 68:17

The chariots of God are twenty thousand, even thousands of angels: the Lord is among them, as in Sinai, in the holy place.

Psalms 68:18

Thou hast ascended on high, thou hast led captivity captive: thou hast received gifts for men; yea, for the rebellious also, that the LORD God might dwell among them.

Psalms 68:19

Blessed be the Lord, who daily loadeth us with benefits, even the God of our salvation. Selah

Zephaniah 3:17

The LORD thy God in the midst of thee is mighty; he will save, he will rejoice over thee with joy; he will rest in his love, he will joy over thee with singing.

Chapter Five

KINGS' HAVE THE PREROGATIVE OF USING ANY GATE

As we come to the end of our discussion, lets pick up from where we left off in the first chapter. If memory serves us right, we said that kings of old had the privilege of using any gate. The gates were entrances and exits to their cities and kingdoms, for example the city of Jericho whose gate was tightly shut with none coming in or going out because of the children of Israel. Similarly, the gate of Samaria was closed because of the Syrians who had besieged the city. Likewise, your life is a City of the Lord whose doors should be kept under consistent surveillance against the enemy of our souls.

When we take a closer look at the way the 'cities' of our lives have been designed and structured by the great Architect of our souls, you will discover that they have five gates, which are the five human senses of taste, smell, touch, hearing and sight. In and through these gates, our King strides to take residence and fulfill His role as Lord of our lives. You may be baffled and wondering how? I will explain in a short while.

It's not enough to know that our King should have unlimited access through the gates in his realm, it is also imperative to recognize the importance and employment of these avenues for his purpose during worship. The beauty and splendor with which God has created us is 'state of the art'. Designed in his likeness and after his similitude, nothing in creation is compared to Man. As spirit beings living in the natural realm, he has given us a soul and a body. Through them, we are able to relate and communicate with other beings and creation via the five senses (gates). I call them gates/doors because they are so. Their primary purpose is for worship. That is what they were mainly designed for by the Master Architect.

Isaiah 43:7
Even every one that is called by my name: for I have created him for my glory, I have formed him; yea, I have made him.

Colossians 1:16 (EMTV).
because by Him all things were created, those in the heavens and those on earth, visible and invisible, whether thrones or dominions or rulers or authorities; all things have been created through Him and for Him.

The moment you and I discover the importance and power in making these gates available for His use, then we will experience His unlimited access into the inner chambers of our cities (lives) effecting healing, provision, salvation, transformation, renewal and restoration. For when He enters unabated, He is bound to do more than we ask or imagine. Your chore (task) is to discern the purpose of your gates and position them in such a way that, whether in private or public worship, your king is Lord in and over your city. Let us have a closer look at each of these gates.

1. GATE OF SMELL;

The faculty of smell is cardinal to Man. It helps you scan the atmosphere and turn away from places contaminated with poisonous odors that may cause suffocation or uneasiness in breathing. On the other hand, coming into contact with scented environments, say, cool morning breezes, a garden of flowers, etc, inspires you to stay a little longer. When employed as a gate of worship, in deep and intense moments of adoration, this faculty may be unlocked to access the beauty of his presence. Since the presence of God is real and tangible, he can choose to manifest it in the physical realm. Ours is to open this vent and if he wills to journey through it, you end up experiencing an environment far different from where you are OR where you are worshipping from. *Ideal worship may allow you experience the air around*

his eternal throne. Before you realize it, the vent that may have been blocked with sinuses, flu virus and any possible nasal cavity infection/ disease is completely transformed. Listen to what the writer says in this portion of scripture.

Songs of Solomon 1:3 (CEV).
And you smell so sweet. All the young women adore you; the very mention of your name is like spreading perfume.

Most of what we see in scripture is a shadow of the reality in heaven. That is why Moses is told to make the ark after the pattern shown to him in the mountain. Heaven is a real place that has its own ambiance. It is awash with tree and plant life of diverse species, all these producing their own scent. That aside, the throne room carries its own 'air' with the smoke of His presence always jetting from the eternal one emitting a unique aroma. Folks, it's very possible for us to occasionally access the atmosphere of His presence via our vent of smell; but ONLY when fine tuned with His Spirit who during worship may give you a heavenly tour, causing you to experience the beauty of paradise. Start making available your gate of smell.

2. GATE OF TOUCH;

Touch is one of the most affectionate modes of communication. It's a language of love, mercy and kindness. Some people respond more to touch than words. A simple touch carries a ton of words. We are known to hug/touch those who are bereaving as a sign of comfort and commiseration; and embrace them in times of joy and happiness. As a gate of worship, it is revealed through the extension of our hands to God. Hands are an integral part of worship. They are an extension of our hearts to God. *The bible speaks about lifting holy hands to God.* Folks, that is why on some occasions, one may experience warmth, electricity, fire, a breeze, etc in their hands when in His presence, because the king is using it as an avenue into His 'city'. One cannot say one is worshiping sufficiently when one's hands, a gate of touch, is out sync with the rest of the body.

In the course of coming through this gate, talking about your King, every debris associated with it such as debt, lack, poverty, habits and financial mishaps is done away with. Before you know it, your hands are cleansed, purified, anointed and garnished with favor. From then on, whatever you touch is blessed, fruitful and multiplies. Items such as money become free flowing through your hands. For those with a zeal to be used of God, the very avenue He uses to come through, is the one He uses to bring healing and deliverance to the captives, as you lay hands on the sick and oppressed. I encourage you to open this gate, my friend. Develop the habit of harmonizing your hands with the rest of your body during worship. It is also a sign of surrender. A symbol that every part of you has been bought with a price and is available for the King's use.

Psalms 63:4
Thus will I bless thee while I live: I will lift up my hands in thy name.

Psalms 134:2
Lift up your hands in the sanctuary, and bless the LORD.

3. GATE OF SIGHT;

One of the hardest defects to cope with is blindness or lack of sight. Even when its partial, it's still uncomfortable. The bible is awash with case scenarios where Jesus healed the blind. One vivid example occurred on his way to Jericho. Bar-timeus while seated begging as was his routine, hears Jesus passing by. He had heard that an itinerant preacher was visiting town and now saw a chance to petition him for help to regain his sight. He howls on the top of his voice saying, Son of David, have mercy on me. Doubtless his vision was restored. Sight helps us appreciate the diverse aspects of creation life surrounding us, but also enables us forge a living in the day to day affairs of life.

When it is duly focused (opened for Him) as a gate of worship, the King may decide to walk through it. The challenge to us is to stay focused during moments of worship. That is why some prefer to have their eyes closed to the surroundings but opened to him! The devil knowing where you are heading, will always strive to disrupt your concentration and make you lose the greatest sight to behold. But when focused (though physically open), the possibility of having open visions of the person of Christ, angels and graphic prophetic messages during that intense moment is high. I repeat, it is very possible to be focused with open eyes!

It's also very likely during times of adoration for God to touch one with impaired vision or limited sight. Others still may behold his glory in different forms; a dove, rain, cloud, fire, etc. These experiences will touch and alter your

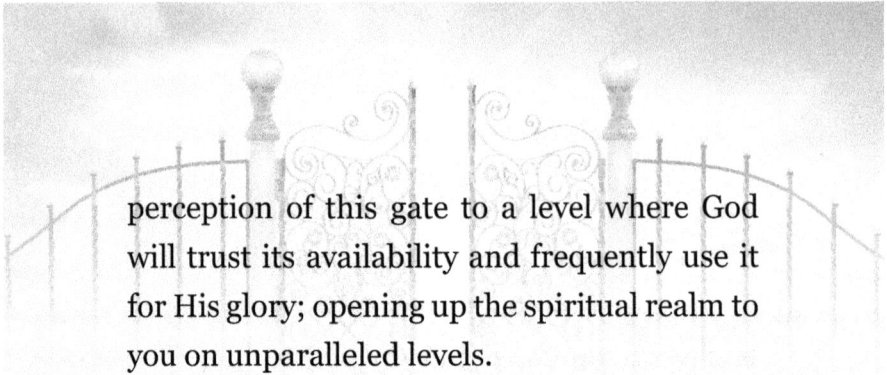

perception of this gate to a level where God will trust its availability and frequently use it for His glory; opening up the spiritual realm to you on unparalleled levels.

Psalms 63:1

O God, thou art my God; early will I seek thee: my soul thirsteth for thee, my flesh longeth for thee in a dry and thirsty land, where no water is;

Psalms 63:2

To see thy power and thy glory, so as I have seen thee in the sanctuary.

4. GATE OF HEARING;

Hearing is vital when it comes to the animal kingdom. For those of you who are nature driven and have a liking to study the animal world or watch documentaries about them, you will learn that animals have distinct sounds. Picture a waddle of penguins by a sea shore. If you are tasked to count them, they may number in the thousands. Time comes when the parents have to go sea shopping to look for food for their young, leaving them on their own. On coming back, a young one (fledgling) may have drifted and wandered from the 'nest' on a site seeing tour. The way the parents are able to call out and recognize their young is through their unique cry sounds. Similarly, wolves live in family structures and every one of those families has a distinct howling sound that identifies a pack or pack-member. Frankly, our human ear cannot decipher their cry sounds.

When translated to the spiritual dimension, the

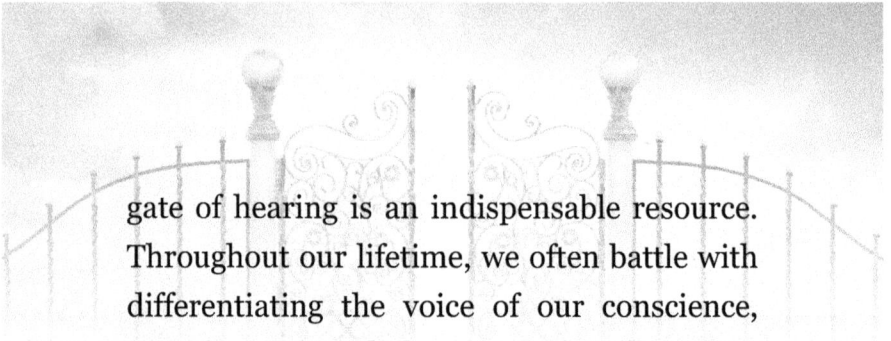

gate of hearing is an indispensable resource. Throughout our lifetime, we often battle with differentiating the voice of our conscience, Satan's voice and the voice of God's Spirit. However, as we turn loose the hinges of this gate God-ward, its frequency is fine tuned and we tap into divine mysteries.

It's been rumored that in times of concentrated worship, people have audibly heard angelic choirs of heaven singing and joined them in adoration. Additionally, through intense engagement of this gate, whatever may have clogged its passage, such as partial deafness and any ear defects, will be obliterated. What you and I need is the voice of God to guide and direct us through the rough terrain of this world. Sessions of worship are a great tool in accessing this priceless treasure. The practice of making available this gate in times of worship will help circumcise it and make the voice of God an integral part of your life.

Recall the experience Saul, Paul of Tarsus had on his way to Damascus to persecute the Christians. He is struck by a light brighter than the midday sun, falls off the beast and hears a voice why are you persecuting me? Those with him heard the voice too and were speechless. In this instance, Jesus crashed through their hearing-gate because he wanted their attention. In worship, he comes through it because it is tuned into him and for him. Again, it is possible to hear an audible voice of God OR a heavenly experience.

Revelation 1:10

I was in the Spirit on the Lord's day, and heard behind me a great voice, as of a trumpet,

Revelation 1:11
Saying, I am Alpha and Omega, the first and the last: and, What thou seest, write in a book, and send it unto the seven churches which are in Asia; unto Ephesus, and unto Smyrna, and unto Pergamos, and unto Thyatira, and unto Sardis, and unto Philadelphia, and unto Laodicea.

5. GATE OF TASTE;

Last but not least, we have the gate of taste, which is a product of our tongue and lips. This small organ is documented by James as able to spread a wild fire. With it, we bless God and curse fellow man. Mis-used and mis-directed it can cause massive destruction. That is why one wise man once wrote, *'death and life are in the power of the tongue and they that love it shall eat of its fruit'*. The beauty of its employment as a gate of worship is evidenced in scripture. Across the pages of his Word when his people put it to right use, God showed up and salvaged them.

When Solomon and the children of Israel were dedicating the temple and the priests were as one to make one sound to praise and thank the LORD, the glory of God came down. Paul and Silas are having a crusade in Philippi, a chief city of Macedonia when they are arrested, flogged and thrown in prison. At midnight they begin praying and singing praises to God who decides to 'crash the party' through an earthquake. Their chains are loosed and the jailer and his family commit to Christ. One of the convicted felons on the cross is agitated with the accusations his counterpart is throwing at the Nazarene. He rebukes him, tells him to halt and gives him an informed view of whom they are crucified with. He acknowledges Jesus as Lord and petitions Him to enroll him as one of the kingdom citizens. Jesus grants his request. Time and space will not suffice to document all the benefits that accrue from the usage of this gate from the biblical stand point.

To maximize its use, we have to look at its functionality in worship. The word of God paints the greatest picture of Him. It describes and details his person and personality exquisitely. With it (word of God), we try to draw mental and spiritual images of him. God and his Word cannot be separated; that is why he has magnified it above all His name. When we tour his word in times of worship, talking about His nature, beauty, greatness and exploits; our language, confession and vocabulary changes AND we begin tasting His attributes in real life. Your destiny is forged from your daily habits, one of which is what you think and say about yourself. ***Worship is the strongest voice of confession.***

In worship, we learn to make the gate of taste available to and for our king. When we do so, He begins to make happen in your life what you are declaring about Him. You can never out give God. That is the meaning of the text below.

Psalms 34:8 (Douay-Rheims Bible).
O taste, and see that the Lord is sweet: blessed is the man that hopeth in him.

Psalms 119:103
How sweet are thy words unto my taste! yea,

sweeter than honey to my mouth!

CONCLUSION

Wait a minute. I hear someone asking, 'does it mean our worship of God is sense driven and not spiritual?' Not at all. Principally worship begins and is centered in our spirit. But while man works his way from outside in; God begins from the inside out. Paul writes to the Corinthians saying, 'Don't you know your body is the temple of the Holy Spirit'? Your life is the official residence of His eternal Spirit. You are also His workmanship. Most times He works in us before He works on our outside.

Philippians 2:13

For it is God which worketh in you both to will and to do of his good pleasure.

Scripture records, 'Enter into his gates with thanksgiving and into his courts with praise'. It also testifies, 'out of your belly shall flow rivers of living water'. The point is, as we endeavor to praise and worship Him, by His choice, we may experience His manifest presence in the outer court of our flesh, the inner court of our soul or the innermost recesses of our spirit. God is not restricted on how and where He manifests himself in us. He is Lord over every zone of our lives. Therefore, our entire frame should exude worship.

Psalms 118:23

This is the LORD'S doing; it is marvellous in our eyes.

Why should it be thought that our tongue/ lips, which is a gate of taste, can help us access spiritual things and other senses (gates) cannot? The one that made the tongue also made the ears, nose and eyes. To Him all can be spiritualized. What turns spiritual these avenues is our faith and availability. For faith is a link between the spiritual and natural realm. It adjoins and creates a correlation between the natural senses and the spiritual sphere in which God dwells. In so doing, there is an overshadowing and eclipsing of His presence and glory touching our spirit, soul and body.

Child of God, open your eyes to the reality of the splendor of your gates and begin utilizing them to the uttermost, so will you see the fulness of His majesty strolling into your City. Fellow citizen of the kingdom, it is time to rise up and take your place. It is time for your City to be radiant with the glory of His presence. As you open all the gates, so will he bless the activities that take place within them.

Psalms 147:13

For he hath strengthened the bars of thy gates; he hath blessed thy children within thee.

BENEDICTION

Ephesians 3:14
For this cause I bow my knees unto the Father of our Lord Jesus Christ,

Ephesians 3:15
Of whom the whole family in heaven and earth is named,

Ephesians 3:16
That he would grant you, according to the riches of his glory, to be strengthened with might by his Spirit in the inner man;

Ephesians 3:17
That Christ may dwell in your hearts by faith; that ye, being rooted and grounded in love,

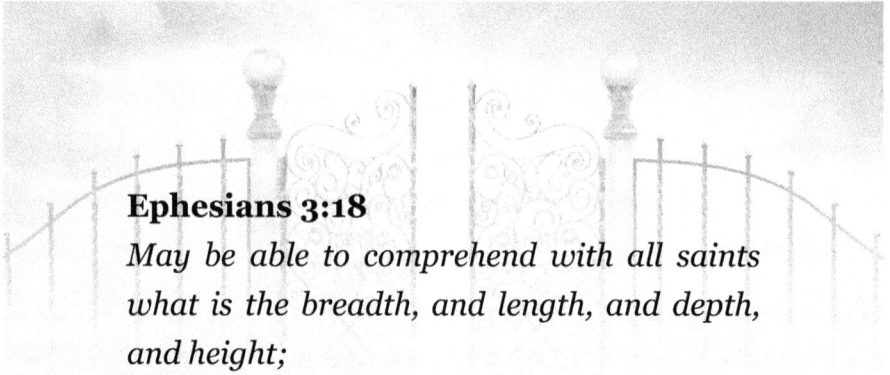

Ephesians 3:18

May be able to comprehend with all saints what is the breadth, and length, and depth, and height;

Ephesians 3:19

And to know the love of Christ, which passeth knowledge, that ye might be filled with all the fulness of God.

Ephesians 3:20

Now unto him that is able to do exceeding abundantly above all that we ask or think, according to the power that worketh in us,

Ephesians 3:21

Unto him be glory in the church by Christ Jesus throughout all ages, world without end. Amen.

Books written:

1. Four Faces of a Worshipper.
2. Worship Keys for Worth-full Living.
3. Gates of Worship.

Coming Soon:

1. Nine Elements of Worship.
2. Composition of Worship.
3. Principles of Faith.
4. Seven Locks of the Anointing.
5. Seven Characteristics of Prayer.
6. Seven Significances of the Cross.

www.ingramcontent.com/pod-product-compliance
Lightning Source LLC
Chambersburg PA
CBHW060655030426
42337CB00017B/2629